The
Y'NEVANO®
Book of
ENCOURAGEMENTS

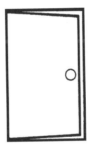

Living a Regretless Life

LAUREEN
No REGRETS

Wali Collins

The Y'NEVANO® Book of Encouragements
Copyright © 2011 by Wali Collins

Cover art by Veronica Rodriguez

ISBN: 978-0-615-46651-4

For more information or for **Y'NEVANO®** products,
Go to: www.ynevano.com

Printed in USA by 48HrBooks (www.48HrBooks.com)

Dedication

This is dedicated to you my parents especially to my mother.

Ma, you said 3 little words to me that brought me incredible success and now I will share with the rest of the world.

Thank you to my mother, Lorraine E. Collins

Table of Contents

Table of Contents

Table of Contents

INTRODUCTION

Y'NEVANO® is a state of mind that will help you to live a regretless life. We all have dreams, goals or desires and sometimes we need a little nudge to get us through any doubt or uncertainty. This book will help you get over any of those obstacles. This book is all about encouraging you to pursue any of those things your spirit is urging you to try. Living in **Y'NEVANO** is so simple to do.

Y'NEVANO is self-empowering and will help you to become more of an independent thinker. Whatever it is you are considering, from changing your hairstyle to mending a relationship, from losing weight to taking on a new career, from getting an education to saying hello to a stranger.

Most importantly, **Y'NEVANO** is saying at the very least, try. It is not about the result of your effort, it is the fact that you made the effort.

Living in the **Y'NEVANO** state of mind will change your life for the better.

The following encouragements are designed to excite your mind and to motivate you to go for any of your dreams.

The choice is yours. Do you want to have a "what if" life or read this book and start living a regretless life?

Y'NEVANO

Perfect Timing

Everyone has his or her own idea of a perfect life. You may think your life is less than perfect meanwhile, someone else may see your life as nothing less than perfect. You may look at someone and wish you had their life because you see it as perfect and all the while they are miserable because they think their life is plain awful. So who is right? What is a perfect life?

Life is going to have its challenges. And everybody has a different life with its own set of challenges. Have you ever known anyone who did not have some kind of challenge in his or her life? No.

And what is better than getting over those challenges and living to talk about it. That is life at its most perfect.

So let us try this again. Look at your life with all of its challenges. Think about those times when you did not think you were going to make it through but somehow you did. You see? Your life is perfect.

Y'NEVANO

You Have No Choice

No matter what, everything you do comes from a choice. **Everything.** As you live, you have to make choices. You choose to get out of bed. You choose what to eat. You choose what clothes to wear. You choose to be happy or sad. You choose to love or hate. You choose to believe or not to believe. You even choose to read these words.

You can change the life you made for yourself if you choose to. Or you can make the choice of staying where you are.

No one, absolutely nobody, can make you feel happy or sad, unworthy or even worthy unless you choose to. It is all up to you to make the choice to believe and react to what that person is saying.

So stop blaming other people for the choices you have made in your life.

The choice is and always will be yours and yours alone.

Y'NEVANO

All About You

We all want to be accepted by our peers, family or even friends. A lot of us do not want to be called out about our differences, because that would put us on the spot or we would have to show our true colors.

Reality check: It is a lot harder trying to "fit in" than just being yourself.

In fact, it is close to impossible. No one is exactly the same when it comes to what we enjoy or what brings us peace. Even identical twins are not the same. There are no laws stating that you must enjoy certain things just because you were born of a certain race or in a certain region. I know what I am saying is not anything you do not know.

Remember those times when you were being you and no one was around to judge you? The world was a beautiful place.

So are you brave enough to allow yourself to be you for the world to see?

Y'NEVANO

Parenting Yourself

Look at your life. Now imagine you are your child. Is this the life you want for him or her? Are you making sure he or she is living a well-rounded life? Keeping him or her from danger, making sure he or she is eating correctly and being on top of any health concerns? Are you making available all the necessary tools to succeed in life? Are you encouraging him or her to go for their dreams or desires?

You are your responsibility. If you look at your life as if it is the life of your child, you would not want to settle for anything less than the best.

Be a great parent to yourself and be proud.

And do not forget to put your accomplishments on the refrigerator.

Y'NEVANO

If Not For You

Where would we be if Beethoven said, "I have these songs in my head but I don't think people want to hear them". Or if Louis Pasteur said, "Why doesn't someone do something about milk tasting so odd?" Or if Carol Burnett said, "I can't do comedy." Or how about if Nelson Mandela said, "Apartheid is wrong but it's not my place to speak out."

But those people did not say those things. They shared their passion and made the world a little nicer of a place to live.

The world needs to experience your passion. It is your responsibility to the world to share what you have. It does not matter how small you think it may be. If it is your passion, it will in some way help. No more of letting someone else try to do what you are great at doing.

So you say, "How can what I'm passionate about help the world?"

All I have for you is one word...

Y'NEVANO

Say It

When was the last time you said, "Thank you" or "I'm sorry" or "I love you" to someone important in your life?

Sometimes those exclusive people are taken for granted and assumed that they are going to be around forever. Some might say that there is no need to say any of that stuff because family and or close friends know it already. Verbalizing what you feel is confirmation of your actions. And there is no guarantee that those significant people are going to be around tomorrow.

Just imagine the feeling of never seeing any of those people again and knowing you never took that moment to express yourself.

Ego or pride has a way of slipping in and prevents you from expressing any of those 3 little phrases. And it will probably take a lot of courage to convey what is in your mind. However, weigh your options. A peaceful conscience or forever thinking about the chances you had.

Y'NEVANO

Did You Hear About So and So?

What is the deal with people gauging their happiness or sadness by other people's success or failures?

Other people's lives have nothing to do with the choices you make for your life. Stop worrying about if Douglas got a new car or if Lillian got fired.

Dwelling on other's fortunes or misfortunes does not benefit your life at all. As a matter of fact, it only takes away from your life. You lose focus of your life goals, dreams or desires wondering what other people are doing.

So as of today, let it be known that you do not have the time to be caught up with other people's lives, because you are busy living your own.

Y'NEVANO

Heartbreak Is A Wonderful Thing

What is with all of this sadness when people get their hearts broken? It really should be a celebration of a confirmation that you can love. To be able to open up and share such a powerful emotion is phenomenal.

To be truly in love is one of those mysteries of the world. You cannot accurately explain the feeling of being in love but you definitely know it when you are in love. It is like trying to describe the smell of a rose in full bloom. Never being in love is like never smelling a rose.

So be happy in the fact that you were capable of unveiling yourself to that euphoric, blissful, titillating, caring, pleasurable, frightening, sensational, awesome, giddy, beautiful, sensitive, thrilling, lustful, frustrating, amazing feeling.

To be in love is all part of living a full life.

So, congratulations on your broken heart.

Y'NEVANO

Ouch Can Be The Truth

It is like getting a shot from a doctor. It may sting at first but whatever is inside that syringe it is designed to cure you from a particular ailment. The truth is designed to cure you from whatever troubles you. At first it may be painful hearing the truth but in time you will benefit from its affirmations.

I recommend that you at least tell the truth to yourself.

Some vaccines require a booster after a few years but the truth will last forever.

Y'NEVANO

Listen And Learn

If you really want to get to know someone, do not say a word, just let him or her talk. People will expose themselves if you give them a chance to express themselves. You will learn all about their ups, downs, fears, passions, likes, dislikes, desires and dreams.

And while you are listening, be careful not to reveal any facial expressions. This is another way of letting that person know that you have an opinion about what they are saying. Just listen and nod your head to let them know that you are hearing what they are saying.

I have learned that people tend to edit their opinions or views if they know you do not see the world just like they do. So being quiet and letting them speak is the key. It will take a lot of restraint not to react to what they say however, discovering what is going on in a person's mind is worth it.

Y'NEVANO someone unless you listen.

Never Before

I am sure you heard, "It's never been done before so, it will never work." Was there ever electricity before electricity was invented? I do not remember reading about people flying before the Wright brothers came along. Someone probably said that the simple little paperclip was a bad idea. And let us not forget about the greatest invention of all time...the wheel.

It has never been done before. That is the meaning of greatness.

So if you have an idea or invention that could change the world for the better, no matter how "crazy" it may seem, go for it. That is exactly what we need, new or better ways to live.

Think about all those other "insane" inventors before you who took on the challenge and did not listen to those people telling them it will never work. They followed a dream and made us all happy for the "crazy" people in the world.

So if you have a "crazy" idea or invention, let us see it. The world needs you.

Y'NEVANO

How Was Your Trip?

That is what people ask after you have made it to your destination. They may give you a hug or a kiss or even a high five for getting there, but the story of how you got there always gets their attention.

It even goes for when you want that certain something really badly. The conversation usually goes something like, "Yeah, I got it but let me tell you what I had to do to get it." The story may be good, bad, funny, crazy, sad, dangerous or even scary. No matter what, it will be intriguing.

So you see? Even though the goal was the reason you got there, how you got there is what you are going to talk about. And if you really think about it, now you have 2 things to look forward to. Getting it or getting there and the story of how you got it or got there.

So, go.

Y'NEVANO

The Lowest Point In Your Life? Impossible.

When you are so convinced that life sucks, consider this, it could be worse. Think of those days when you felt like life had punched you in the gut, it always could have been worse.

No matter how "bad" you believe it is, it could be worse.

There is no such thing as "the lowest point in your life" because you can always go lower.

So instead of focusing and getting depressed on how bad you think life is, take joy in knowing it is not as worse as it could be.

Y'NEVANO

Lazy Is Expensive

I see it all the time. Choosing not to caulk the windows for the winter, just paying the high heating bill. Not flossing and then dealing with oral surgery. Not washing your clothes just buying new ones.

It is the knowing that you can do better but choose not to, which you know will cost you in the end.

Laziness is the easiest trap of all traps. All you have to do is, nothing.

I really think people do not realize how laziness can cost more than money. Being lazy can cost friends, family or more importantly, your life.

Y'NEVANO

A Fish Life

Ever look at fish in an aquarium? They just swim around with not much direction. Just content being where they are and accepting their surroundings. This is how their world was, is and always will be. That is the best those fish lives are going to be.

If you have not tried to go for any of your passions, dreams or desires, and believe that this is the best your life is going to be, you are one of those fish in that aquarium. Just moving around the earth aimlessly until you die.

This is your life. YOUR LIFE. You have the power to take yourself out of that small, cramped mental aquarium and place yourself in a big, beautiful deep blue sea of possibilities or opportunities by simply going for your dreams.

Y'NEVANO

Worth A Thousand Words

If you really are not into writing or logging entries into a diary or a life journal, take pictures of yourself.

That's right. Take pictures of yourself when you feel you are going through challenging times. And do not write or log anything of what you are dealing with on the photo. Let the photo speak for itself. This will help you for 2 reasons:

1) When you go back to look at the photos you have taken, you will relive what you were going through and see that you made it to the other side of whatever it was.

2) When you go back to look at your photos, you may not even remember why you took those pictures. And you are going to see that your problems were not as bad as they seemed.

Your photo diary/journal is just for you and no one else.

So when you are troubled, take a picture of yourself. Later you will literally see that you can get through any of your problems, struggles or dilemmas.

Y'NEVANO

Haters + Bullies = Success

Haters are those people that do not want you to succeed. They are jealous of your accomplishments or something that you possess. They will say and do things to you to make them feel better about what they think they are lacking in their lives.

Yes, some call these kinds of people bullies. Bullies are insecure with themselves. So in their minds, in order for them to feel better about themselves they must equalize the playing field. They will try to make you feel insecure about yourself or try to take away whatever you have.

In other words, you must be doing something right if people are jealous of you. These people envy you and they cannot handle it.

So let these haters or bullies come your way and use them as your scorecard as to how well you are doing.

The more come your way, the better your score.

Y'NEVANO has haters and it gives me pride.

Road Trip

Remember when you were a kid in the car going on a fantastic outing and your parents used turning the car around as a form of discipline? You were not exactly sure what was going to be there but from the stories you had heard it was going to be a good time. Thinking about how much fun you were going to have and the threat of missing out on all of that was just plain scary.

Grown ups knew that turning back would be so disappointing to you. You knew what was back there at home, same old toys, same old food and same old people. Yuk!

Remember all the anticipation you had about getting to that place? That is the same attitude you should have when you are going for your goals or desires. You are on your way to living your dream. The thought of going back to where you came from should be horrifying, frustrating and frankly a huge let down.

Y'NEVANO

(And when you get there, do not even think about going back.)

Other People's Dreams

As I go through life, I ask the people I know what their dreams are. I am always surprised at what they say. My dad, the marine, always dreamed of doing voiceover for radio. My grandfather, the electrician, always wanted to be an airline pilot. My sister, who works at a daycare, wishes to be a car mechanic. My accountant wants to be a stand up comedian.

Try this with your family and friends. You will be fascinated by some of their answers. Use this exercise to be your motivator. You can use the choices they did not make for their lives as the inspiration for you to live your dream(s).

And maybe just maybe they will see you living your dream and that will encourage them to go for theirs.

Y'NEVANO people no matter how well you know them.

Alone? Never

Ever have those days when you are so sure that you are going through something all by yourself? You are convinced that no one else can possibly relate to what you are feeling. There is no doubt in your mind that your situation is just that unique.

No matter how singular you may feel, there is someone out there that can relate to you or has already been where you are going. There is a person on this planet taking the same journey as you.

If need be, you can reach out to support groups, certain public venues or events.

An island is a body of land which stands alone but remember, there are many islands.

The truth is that you do not have to go through whatever it is all by yourself.

Y'NEVANO

Challenge!

Here is a great way to get yourself out of your present state of mind and into the Y'NEVANO state of mind.

Challenge yourself.

Make up little fun challenges for you against yourself and try to improve on them as you go along.

*Challenge yourself to hold your breath for a full 5 minutes. You probably cannot do it on your first try. So that means you would have to keep trying until you do.

*How about the challenge of trying to remember everybody's first name at the next party you are invited to? If you can do that, you will impress a lot of people.

*Recite the alphabet from Z to A as fast as you can.

*Learn how to say "Hello" in every language possible.

*Look at all of the red or blue or green things in the room, and then with your eyes closed, say what they are by memory.

It is you in competition with yourself. This is a great way of putting yourself on that path to living in Y'NEVANO.

It Is A Fact

There is a popular saying that states we all can't be winners. Which is a fact. That means everyone cannot win. And if you believe everyone cannot win, it stands to reason that everyone cannot lose either. Which would also be a fact.

Ok. So with that understanding, the next time you have any doubts when going for any of your dreams, goals or desires, remind yourself of the fact that we all cannot be losers.

Which means it is a fact that quite possibly YOU are going to win.

Y'NEVANO

Safe And Secure

You know those situations when you are all nervous and flustered and you need to calm down? People may suggest for you to close your eyes and imagine yourself on a sandy beach or put yourself in a meadow with green grass and...blah, blah, blah.

That does not work for everybody. In fact some people may get even more flustered because they do not have that kind of creative ability.

When you need to relax your brain for whatever reason, go for what you know. Just think of the times when you felt the safest. Those moments of feeling secure and just knowing everything was all right.

For instance, think of the times your grandmother hugged you when you were a child. Knowing that your rent was paid for the month. Enjoying Thanksgiving dinner with friends and family. Or doing absolutely nothing with the one you adore. Thinking about the times you felt the safest will immediately put your mind at ease.

If you want to relax, don't imagine just remember.

Y'NEVANO

The Meaning Of The Word "No"

Giving up on your dreams does not make sense to me. Just because you get a "NO" does not mean that is it, pack it up or stop pursuing your goal.

What "NO" really means is, "There is another way".

Getting to your goal is exactly like going through the maze you find in children's magazines. You start off on your path. This is a path of your choosing. If that path is blocked, what do you do? Do you say, "That's it. I can't go any further.", give up and throw the magazine in the trash? No, not at all. What you do is just simply back up a little and start another path. And if your path is blocked again, you just keep backing up taking new paths until you reach your goal.

Sometimes those "NO's" can help guide you to reach your goal a lot sooner.

Y'NEVANO

Why?

Why do you eat those foods? Why do you hang out with those friends? Why do you wear those clothes? Why do you...?

Have you ever asked yourself why you do the things you do? Most of the time we do things because we were taught or told to do them. You probably do not even like doing some of those things but you do them anyway out of habit.

I dare you to challenge yourself by asking, "Why do I do the things I do?"

Y'NEVANO. You could be missing out on a whole new way of doing things.

Anti vs. Pro

Ok. This is a tricky one.

Achieving a goal is all in how you view it. If you do not like being broke all the time, do not think anti-poor think **pro**-rich. If you are depressed, try to be **pro**-happy not anit-sad. Looking for that special someone? Anti-single is not going to work. You have to be **pro**-relationship. Teach your children **pro**-smart is better than anti-dumb. Not getting along with a family member? Anti-argue? No. **Pro**-getting along? Yes. Never anti-fat. Go for **pro**-healthy.

It is about being in the affirmative frame of mind. Being anti-anything keeps you thinking about where you do not want to be. Being **pro**-something is keeping your thoughts in that place where you need to be.

And lastly, do not be anti-staying in my mundane life be **pro**-change my life for the better.

Y'NEVANO

What's With The Kindness?

I have seen people actually get mad because they did not get a "thank you" for holding the door for someone.

So what you did not get a thank you. You held that door because you felt like doing something nice. You were not asked to hold the door. You did it from the kindness of your heart. If you voluntarily do a favor you should not be looking for any kind of gratification. Watching someone taking advantage of your favor should be gratification enough. Expecting appreciation for your "selfless" act is not much of a selfless act. It is more like a "self" act.

So the next time you hold a door for someone or let someone cut ahead of you or pick up something that someone dropped, make sure you know the reason why.

Y'NEVANO

That Certain Person

There is that certain person. You see them everyday. You do not know his or her name. You do not know his or her background. You really do not know the specifics about them at all. But for some reason he or she has your attention. It might be the way they dress or the way they speak or the confidence they may have by the way he or she carries his or herself. And they have no idea that you have noticed them. As time goes on, you start to wonder the kind of life he or she has. Are they rich or poor? What is their family history? What are their values? Then you realize that you have taken time out of your life to think about someone you do not know. It is pretty powerful how someone you do not know can affect you.

Here is a thought. **You** could be that certain person to someone.

So be the best **you** you can be.

Y'NEVANO who you are impressing.

Celebrate Good Times Right Now

Why do we wait for something "big" to happen in order to celebrate?

If you keep that up, you are going to miss out on great opportunities to celebrate. Celebrate that you are alive. Celebrate the fact that it is just an ordinary day. Celebrate your enemies. Celebrate celebrating. When I say celebrate, I mean really do it up. I'm talking black tie, gown, champagne, music, friends and family.

Celebrating is fun and so necessary to keep our lives exciting.

Y'NEVANO how much you appreciate things in life until you celebrate them.

Beginner's Luck Is A Myth

Ever notice how people win at gambling or a sport they try for the first time? Some will call that "Beginner's Luck". I love it when the people who have been at it for years get so furious. They say things like, "He had no idea what he was doing and yet he won!!"

There is no such thing as "Beginner's Luck". The reason why those people win is because they are so focused on the end result. WINNING. Nothing else. That is the purest form of focus anyone can ask for.

Experienced people use strategy to win games. What they are actually telling themselves is that they might lose. The focus on the end result is not at its purest anymore. They are too busy thinking how to avoid ways that could make them not win.

There is a big difference in focusing on not losing the game and focusing on winning the game.

Y'NEVANO

Unfinished Work

When was the last time you started a personal project and finished it? Such as doing away with clothes you do not wear anymore, organizing your important home documents, getting rid of your kids old toys, learning how to work that universal remote control, fixing that door, insulating around the windows, painting that room, writing the letter and sending it or cleaning out that old junk drawer.

I am sure you have reasons why you are not finishing those projects. But you not finishing says a lot more about you than those things not getting done.

Maybe that is why you have not reached those other goals or dreams you set for yourself. It is because you have lost your focus.

Actually finishing one of those mundane projects can be a great way to practice your focus.

And feel great knowing that you have finished what you set out to do.

Y'NEVANO

The Power Of A Penny

I sometimes see people actually throw pennies on the ground as if those coins were trash. When I see money on the ground, I pick it up. Yes, even pennies. A penny is currency. It has value.

To me, pennies are like human beings. One person may not be able to do much but, if you put a lot more together, they can make a difference. Strength in numbers applies to pennies too. Put enough together and you have got a nickel or a dime or even a quarter.

I mean think about it. Think of all the pennies that you have passed by or waved off as change from your purchases. Who knows how much money you could have had.

Y'NEVANO

Your Advice

If you could go back in time to when you were 6 years old, what advice would you give yourself?

If you could go back in time to when you were 12 years old, what advice would you give yourself?

What advice would you give yourself at 18?

What advice would you give yourself if you went back in time to yesterday?

What advice would you give yourself for tomorrow?

By the way, make sure Y'NEVAVO is part of your advice for tomorrow.

Y'NEVANO

Take Inventory

In order to get more from your life you have to appreciate what you have already.

When was the last time you stopped and looked at all of the great things you have in your life? Some may say, "I have nothing in my life to be happy about". And I say, "Really?"

First, let us start with the simple stuff or the things you take for granted, like the breath in your lungs or the ability to read this. And then there are the clothes you are wearing. Next, move up to the friends and family, those people who came to your aid when you needed it.

Now that I have gotten you started in itemizing the stock in your life, you probably can think of a few more things to be happy about.

Take the time and take inventory of all the gifts in your life.

Y'NEVANO, your inventory list could be endless.

Failure Is Better Than Success

The most common reason why people do not succeed is because they are afraid of the unknown.

When you succeed you are putting yourself in a place where you have never been. These new places may appear scary and intimidating. So instead you stay where you are. Do not grow or move up or do anything that would change your environment. This is your comfort zone. Even though it may be an unhappy place, you know it and what to expect from it.

Look at it like this. If you were put in prison, all you would want to do is escape if you had the chance. What would you do or where would you go? You would go anywhere or do anything as long as you are not in captivity anymore.

Not letting yourself succeed is putting you in your own prison.

Do what you can to get out of your prison. Educate yourself, say yes to different opportunities or even try networking in different circles.

It is your choice to be free or let your life rot away in captivity.

Y'NEVANO

Go Ahead And Brag

What is it that you can brag about?

Your kids? Your income? A certain body part? Your pet? Your collections? Running a marathon? Your home? Your talent?

Bragging is just putting your pride on display. You are so proud of something that you cannot hold it in. You are so proud that you must tell the world or anybody who is willing to listen. And when you think or look at what you are proud of, you get a feeling of satisfaction.

So use that satisfied feeling when insecurity starts to creep into your mind. Remember that no matter what, you can always be proud of...(*Insert what you want to brag about here*)

Y'NEVANO

The Good Old Days? I Don't Think So

What was it about the old days to call them good? From what I have read in the history books people had it pretty rough back then. The Inquisition, scarlet fever, slavery, the Holocaust, life expectancy was a lot shorter, people could smoke cigarettes on a plane, and worst of all, rotary phones.

Things are a lot different now. We as a people are more conscious about our health, we are living longer lives, we can get an answer to any question by going on to the internet, casual Fridays at work, and of course, touchtone phones.

To me, life is looking pretty good as time goes on. I am not going to try to kid myself and think that everything is great. I know there are still some things this world has to work on. But for the most part, I can say without any doubt that things are changing for the better.

So leave the "good old" days behind and enjoy the better days ahead. And with that understanding, know that everyday is going to get better.

Y'NEVANO the beauty tomorrow will bring.

Talk To Yourself...

...And listen to what you have to say. A lot of times I am able to solve my own problems just by talking to myself OUT LOUD. I know it sounds crazy or weird but it really works. Sometimes we internalize our situations inside our minds and not let those issues see the light of day.

It is very gratifying to listen to yourself as if you are your own Therapist. As a Therapist, you want to help your patient get clarity and enjoy a satisfying life. Take in all the information you tell yourself OUT LOUD. Weigh the options and tell yourself the best way to handle the problem OUT LOUD.

Do this a few times and after a while you will be able to separate you from yourself and be able to look at things from a different angle. Do it a few more times and you will swear there are 2 people in the room.

Y'NEVANO. If you are good enough, you can charge yourself $200 an hour.

Live A Regretless Life

There is an R&B song called, "If I, Coulda, Woulda, Shoulda". Those are the words of regret. How many times have you said one of those words because you missed out on an opportunity?

Having any regrets is just wishing to change the past. It is a waste of time. We all know you cannot change yesterday.

Let today be the first day of your Regretless Life. If the opportunity is there, go for it. Just start with the small things and build up.

Here are some suggestions to help get you started:

*Try a new recipe. *Wear a color you never wore before. *Go half a day without using your cell phone. *Understand that you do not have to win every argument. *Find a math problem and solve it. *Send a letter not an email. *Give that music you hate an honest chance. *Volunteer your time.

Let today be the first day of the rest of your life when you can say without any doubt, "I have a regretless life."

Y'NEVANO, you might even start to smile more.

Mmmm

Why do we season our food? Because we do not want to eat a bland meal. Every once in a while we need to spice things up. It is exciting having the different flavors bouncing around in our mouths.

Same thing goes for life. It is time to add some seasoning. Start small or simple like just with salt and pepper or sugar. Then move up to some garlic. Continue on to cinnamon or curry. And then you can make that jump to cayenne. Try one at a time or maybe mix some of the spices together.

Adding flavors to your life is not only exciting, it is delicious.

Y'NEVANO how tasty life can be.

That One Thing

What is that one thing you could do for hours? The thing you feel you were born to do. What is that particular something that when you are doing it, it brings you peace and a certain calmness? My question to you is why are you not doing it all the time? Is it because you have other responsibilities or a job?

Believe it or not, you can make a career out of whatever your passion is.

Think about it. If we all did our passion as a career, we would not feel any stress about getting our 40 hours in or angry because we have to do over-time. Waking up to go to work would be a great thing. Some of us would never retire.

We are meant to live our lives doing what we love to do, not what we are "suppose" to do.

Just imagine getting paid for doing something you love.

Y'NEVANO how happy you could be.

Dreams Don't Come True

I hear it all the time. "Why won't my dreams come true?". "I wish with all my heart and nothing." or "I put the goals that I dream for in my Y'NEVANO box and no success".

You have these wishes and dreams and goals for a better life. Sometimes you even imagine yourself in front of the mirror being or doing what you wish for but only for a few minutes before returning to your "real life". There is the problem. You do not believe **you are** what you wish for.

Let me explain. If you want to be a photographer, you have to eat, sleep, drink, and live like a photographer. In other words, be a photographer 24/7. Or how about starting your own business? Warren Buffet or Sir Richard Branson or even Oprah do not wish to be rich and successful. They know that they are rich and successful. Want to lose weight? You have to believe you are a healthy thin person.

Know without any doubt that you are whatever it is and your actions will follow.

I promise, YOU WILL SUCCEED.

Y'NEVANO

When Was The Last Time...

...you laughed so hard your body was on the verge of collapsing. The sound coming out of your mouth was not your normal "HA-HA". It was something unrecognizable. The cheeks on your face literally ached. You could not see clearly because your eyes were blurry from the tears. That pain in your belly was unbearable. You were desperately trying to catch your breath and you worried for a second you might pass out.

It is so ironic to be in such physical misery while having one of the best moments in your life.

So take a minute and think about the last time you laughed like that. I am sure it will at least put a smile on your face.

And for anyone who cannot remember when or never experienced laughing like that, all I can say is, and as crazy as it may sound...

Y'NEVANO how great life is until you laugh so hard to the point of agony.

Principle Of "JUMP"

In order to jump, which will bring you to a higher plain, you must first lower yourself.

To jump successfully you must follow these simple steps:

Step 1: Bend your knees. This collects energy for your jump.

Step 2: Quickly push your body up springing off of your feet.

Use this analogy to better yourself in a career, sports or a change in lifestyle.

First, you need to look to see where or how far you need to jump. Next, get knowledge, information, education or the training necessary. It may seem like you are pulling yourself away from your goal. On the contrary, this is considered the bending at the knees part. You are collecting the energy needed for your jump. Then when you feel you have acquired all the necessary tools, you make that jump by pushing yourself into that new world.

There is no other way to jump. You have to follow that rule to get up there.

Y'NEVANO how high you can jump.

A Left Instead

It was a nice day here in New York City. So I decided to start my day a bit earlier and go the long way to the subway. Instead of the right turn as soon as I leave the building, I decided to take a left turn. I have to admit, just by going in the opposite direction I felt a sense of freedom. With this liberating feeling, it seemed like everything was new to me. I noticed children playing across the street. I realized that there were not as many cars passing on the road. I was even saying, "Hello" or "Good morning" or "Nice day, huh?" to the people I passed by. And then, I saw a new bakery that sold my favorite of all things to eat, chocolate chip cookies. I bought 2 cookies and enjoyed them as I finished my journey to the A train.

This story is not just about the children or the lack of cars or even the cookies. It is about the feeling I felt while noticing those things. It was just by simply deciding to take that left turn.

Y'NEVANO unless you try.

Prevention Is The Best Health Plan

Why do we ignore the little reminders for staying in good health?

The doctors tell us to eat more fruits and vegetables. It is recommended to take the stairs not the escalator when possible. Adults are told to take an extra 2 minutes in the shower to check for any unfamiliar lumps or bumps because, early detection of testicular or breast cancer is important. Do not smoke cigarettes. Even the dentist tells us to floss everyday. Why? So our teeth do not fall out of our heads.

It is proven and we all know this as a fact that if we do these SIMPLE things (I cannot stress SIMPLE enough) chances are we will live a lot longer to enjoy time with friends, family and our favorite TV shows.

Remember, laziness is very expensive.

Y'NEVANO

Too Old? Shut Up!

"I can't because, I'm too old". That is not a good enough reason to stop you from going for your dream. Oh sure, younger people have resiliency when they make a mistake. They have that ability to pop right back up when they fall. But there is a certain kind of belief or faith with older people that only comes with age.

*George Foreman won the WBC heavyweight championship at 45.

*Maria del Carmen Bousada was 66 years old when she gave birth to twins.

*At 42, Rodney Dangerfield quit his job as a paint salesman to become a stand up comedian.

*Great-great grandmother Gustava Bennett Burrus got her high school diploma at the age of 97.

Those are just a few people that did not see age as a reason not to try. So now let those people motivate you to go for yours.

It is still out there waiting for you.

Y'NEVANO

Children

Who would have thought the youngest boy of four children, would grow up to be the leading force in getting his country's independence. That's right, Gandhi has inspired so many people. People such as Dr. Martin Luther King, Jr.

Who would have thought a little girl who was abused by her step grand parents would grow up to be the first female millionaire TV executive. Not only did Lucille Ball make us all laugh but she was also an incredible businesswoman.

Here is my point. The man who invented pasteurization was a child. The first brain surgeon was a child. Even your favorite teacher from elementary school was a child. So be careful what you say or do to those little snotty nose, noise making and disobedient young people. For he or she could be the one who invents gas-less cars, who cures the common cold or who finds the key to world peace.

Y'NEVANO

Never Under Estimate...

...the power of taking a deep breath.

It amazes me how we take the most basic things for granted.

I have been advised to take a deep breath when I am confused or sad or when I am at my wits end. Taking a breath helps you to get focused again. It is a "Zen-like" way to clear one's mind.

But have you ever taken a deep breath when life is at its best? When you see a rainbow, watch your child take her first step or go into the post office and there is no line. It is truly an indescribable feeling. There is something about filling your lungs up with air and slowly letting it out. It is like a quick mini-meditation.

The nice thing about it is that it does not cost anything. You can do it almost anywhere. And people will not look at you funny when you do it.

So go ahead. Take a deep breath right now...

It's ok. I'll wait...

Nice, right?

Y'NEVANO

At The Very Least

So many of us are afraid of living our dream for whatever reason.

Imagine you lying on your deathbed or you taking your last breath. I know this may be very morbid but it is going to happen. However, what do you think is going to be going through your mind besides who will show up at your funeral? It is those things you always wanted to try.

Seeing the Eiffel Tower, standing in Times Square, tasting the salt water from the Tasman Sea, learning how to salsa, shaving your head, streaking, telling your boss what you really think, squashing old beefs, getting regular check ups, saying yes or saying no for that matter, or even doing absolutely nothing at all.

Y'NEVANO is designed to have no regrets. All Y'NEVANO is saying is, TRY IT.

Do not get hung up on the result of your trying. It is all about knowing that you can say to yourself, "The most important thing I did was try".

Y'NEVANO

Believing Or Knowing

This is an easy one.

Would you want to believe you have won the lottery or would you want to know you have won the lottery? There is a bridge of uncertainty involved when it comes to believing but, you are standing on solid ground when you are knowing.

The reason why we wear seat belts is that we believe we could be in an accident because, we know if we are, it will not be a good thing.

Ever hear about athletes being in the "zone" and that is how they won the game? It is because they already know they won even before the game started.

That is the kind of thinking you need when you make the decision to change your life for the better.

Believing that you are going to reach your goal is not going to cut it. You have to KNOW it.

Y'NEVANO how strong you can be.

Legacy

What is your legacy? What is that thing or things that will carry on your spirit and or your beliefs after you leave this planet? What is that something you have put your heart and soul into? It could be your children or your high score at the video arcade or a recipe of your own design.

It is such a waste of anyone's life to just exist. You are here for a reason. Show how your life was worth something.

*Plant trees.
*Teach what you know to others.
*Come up with a catch phrase.

Do something that shows the world that you were here and you lived a life.

Your legacy will speak of you long after you are gone.

Y'NEVANO

ABOUT THE AUTHOR

Wali Collins is the founder and CEO of Y'NEVANO Inc. He was born in Springfield, Massachusetts. The youngest of 3 children and the only boy, he had a lot of ambition and imagination as a child. Growing up he loved to paint pictures and would sell his work to family and friends. At the age of 12 Wali organized the first dog competition in his neighborhood. A love for music led to Wali learning to play the drums and becoming the youngest member of the New England Jazz Society.

He studied architectural technology in college and was content on designing buildings until the urge to be a standup comedian came along. Through a successful comedy career, he has traveled the world, hosted TV shows and had the honor of performing in events with 2 American presidents.

Y'NEVANO has helped Wali to succeed in all facets of his life. He feels a responsibility to share what he has discovered with the world. Wali realized the best way to help people get into the Y'NEVANO state of mind, was to come up with a product line and other tactics that will encourage people to go for their dreams.

For more information, to become a member of the social network or to purchase any other **Y'NEVANO**® motivational devices, go to www.ynevano.com.